Ella's Dragon

Written by
Cath Jones

Illustrated by
Ryan Ball

CLANK! BANG! THUD!

Ella was working in her shed. She had made another new robot.

"Ella!" called the queen. "It's time for you to go and learn how to be a brave knight."

"Oh Mum!" said Ella. "Do I have to? You know I don't want to kill dragons."

"Yes, you must!" said Mum.

On the first day of knight school, Ella was sent on a quest.

"Go and find a dragon to fight," said the teacher.

Ella looked on top of a big hill. No dragon.

She looked in a huge, old cave. No dragon.

She even looked in the castle, just in case. But everywhere she looked, there were no dragons.

"Mum will not be happy if I don't find a dragon," Ella thought.

Ella spent the weekend in her shed.

CLANK! BANG! THUD!

She made a robot dragon!

It had a very loud roar and red hot fire came out of its mouth.

Ella called her dragon Clara. It was very cute!

But on Monday …

… Knock, knock, knock.
There was a dragon outside the shed!

"My name is Bob. I have come to see Clara. She looks so cute!" said Bob.

When the people in the castle saw Bob, they ran away in fright.

"Fight that dragon!" said the queen to Ella.

Ella hid Clara and Bob behind her shed. They were very happy together.

But word spread about Clara. Other dragons came to meet her!

The queen was very unhappy. All the people in the castle had run away and no one came to see her for tea, because of the dragons.

"Ella, you need to fight the dragons," said the queen. "Come on, it's your duty!"

"I don't want to hurt any of these lovely dragons," thought Ella.

She went back to her shed.

CLANK! BANG! THUD!

Ella came out of the shed in her knight's outfit. She went out to the dragons and they had a long chat.

A little later, all of the dragons flew away. Ella went back to her shed.

Then the queen came out of her castle and the people slowly crept back.

Suddenly, Clara the robot dragon landed.

A moment later, a knight came out of Ella's shed. It looked just like Ella.

The knight and Clara had a huge, fantastic battle.

Nobody won, but the queen was pleased. Ella was fighting a dragon!

"Well done, Ella!" called the queen.

Nobody ever found out that Clara and the knight were both robots!